Images of
McCall

Valley County
and beyond

Right: Marina reflections, Payette Lake.
© **CHAD CASE \ IDAHO STOCK IMAGES**

Front cover and title page: Wooden boat show,
Payette Lake. **GARY ERTTER**

Back cover: Ponderosa Park. **TED DEMETRIADES**

For more information about this book,
please visit us at www.McCall-DonnellyEducationFoundation.org
or write P.O. Box 3048, McCall, ID 83638

McCall-Donnelly
EDUCATION
FOUNDATION

Parents and citizens in the McCall-Donnelly area have formed the McCall-Donnelly Education Foundation to raise funds and resources to support academic and enrichment programs within the McCall-Donnelly School District. The Foundation operates independently of the School District, but works closely with it as an active partner in enhancing our schools' programs.

The McCall-Donnelly Education Foundation salutes the contributors listed below. Thanks to the generosity of these donors, the publishing costs of *Images of McCall, Valley County and Beyond* have been entirely underwritten. Therefore, all proceeds from the sale of this book will be directed to local school programs.

William R. Eldredge
President

Principal Underwriter:

WHITETAIL
CLUB & RESORT

Major Contributor:

JUG MOUNTAIN RANCH
McCALL, IDAHO

Significant Contributors: Bill and Molly Eldredge
Jean Odmark

Supporting Sponsors: The Andrew J. Bernstein Foundation
Wolfe and Julie Ashcraft – Pro Peak Sports
Tim Garber – The Mill Restaurant
Ron and Diana Sabala
Ballard and Loree Smith
Tamarack Resort

Ski bike fish swim play
Winter Spring Summer or Fall
McCall has it all.

RYAN STOUFFER
GRADE 9

Welcome to McCall. © CHAD CASE \ IDAHO STOCK IMAGES

I can go fishing and will catch a fish,
Then I will go home,
I will eat the fish.

MORGAN PALMERTON
GRADE 1

A great catch, Mountain Lake. **ROBERT MONROE**

Foxes
Wild, playful,
mammals, noisy, beautiful,
speedy, clever
foxes.

ELLIE TERHERST
GRADE 2

Fox on Aspen Ridge. **TRIXI HUISH**

Tan, white-tailed,
Fast, quiet, wild, herds,
Smart deer.

AVON VAN NOY
GRADE 2

Deer, Ponderosa Park. **TRIXI HUISH**

Winter at Jug Mountain Ranch.
KEVIN ELLIOTT/JUG MOUNTAIN RANCH

Future Olympians at Jug Mountain Ranch. **KEVIN ELLIOTT/JUG MOUNTAIN RANCH**

Right: McCall Curling Club. **MATT MOEHR**

Below: Ice skating, Peter Pan Ice Show. **JO ELLEN YRIBAR**

Free-skating on smooth ice
Unlocks my mind.

ALINA EVERETT
GRADE 10

Crowds screaming
Players skating rapidly
Goal!
We win! Hockey, love it.

LINDSEY HALL
GRADE 5

Heartland Youth Hockey. **MATT MOEHR**

Manchester Ice and Event Center, McCall. **TED DEMETRIADES**

Winter lights, Hotel McCall. **JOY HAMILTON**

Evening view downtown, Cascade. **HOWARD HAMILTON**

Little Ski Hill building. **KATY SABALA**

I love to ski with my family so much,
and then we eat at the lodge.

EMMA SABALA
GRADE 1

Little Ski Hill, McCall. **KATY SABALA**

Excitement grows strong
As glistening white ceases flight
Gently in the night.

SAM RAINEY
GRADE 9

Little Ski Hill, McCall. **GARY ERTTER**

Flames licking the air
Sparks dueling in the darkness
It's a boy's night out.

RYAN McKENZIE
GRADE 8

Fourth of July, Brown Park. **GARY ERTTER**

I love to watch the rodeo
Horses are running
Cows are mooing
Goats are talking
A rodeo is the place for me!

BREANNA ELLIS
GRADE 2

Budding calf roper, Valley County Rodeo. **GARY ERTTER**

Hang in there Buddy! Mutton Bustin' at the Valley County Rodeo. **GARY ERTTER**

Bull rider in the making, Valley County Rodeo. **GARY ERTTER**

Above: Steer Wrestling, Council. **GARY ERTTER**

Facing page: Senior Pro Rodeo, Council. **GARY ERTTER**

Old barns. **TRIXI HUISH**

Very fast, very tall,
They gallop and run,
They eat hay,
You ride on a saddle,
Pull on the reins,
You will want to stay on
Until bedtime.

KALIE HAYNES
GRADE 2

Little Rodeo Rider. **GARY ERTTER**

The shining sunset
Makes the plains gleam with color
And look quite peaceful.

NICK WRIGHT
GRADE 4

The sun was setting,
It looked like it was for me.

TAUNA NELSON
GRADE 4

Valley County sunset.
© STEVE BLY \ IDAHO STOCK IMAGES

49

Fall leaves, McCall. **MOLLY ELDREDGE**

Beautiful crimson
Leaves fall to the ground gently
Leaving me in awe.

ALYSSA AMORT
GRADE 9

Color floating down
Wind whipping them all around
Resting on the ground.

SOPHIA BALDRICA
GRADE 9

Brown Park, McCall. TED DEMETRIADES

Early morning mist, Payette Lake. HOWARD HAMILTON

The icy lake reflects the scenery, like an unseen mirror
Clouds quietly roll aside.

ASHTYN GONZALEZ
GRADE 8

A quiet moment, Payette Lake. **JOY HAMILTON**

I remember as a child,
I could hardly endure the wait.
Everyday in March, after the snow started to melt and flow
down the majestic tops of the mountains,
I would wander down to the beach.
Kneeling down to where my eyes met the water,
I would place my tiny finger in the blood of the mountain.
I would return disappointed and confused.
The sun had not yet reached my expectations.

MEGAN DAVIS
GRADE 8

The morning has come
White fluff is everywhere to see
It is time to ski.

SKYLER GULLICKSON
GRADE 9

Off the cornice at Tamarack Resort. **GARY ERTTER**

Original Brundage Mountain Ski Lodge. **COURTESY OF ANN LLOYD EDWARDS**

Brundage Mountain Ski Lodge. **GARY ERTTER**

"Lyda" on Payette Lake. **COURTESY OF TIM GARBER**

Car passing through high snow bank. **COURTESY OF TIM GARBER**

Downtown McCall Hotel. **COURTESY OF JAYNE BROWN**

Shore Lodge.
COURTESY OF ANN LLOYD EDWARDS

Boating on Payette Lake.
COURTESY OF ANN LLOYD EDWARDS

Dorothy Brown Beyerle on chair lift. COURTESY OF SUSAN REAVES AND AMY PEMBERTON

Super Pipe, Tamarack Resort. **GARY ERTTER**

2005 USCSA Nationals at Brundage Mountain. **GARY ERTTER**

Snowboarding rocks me
Fresh powder, friends, jumps, rails
Best time of my life.

KELSEA MOORE
GRADE 9

I can explore.
First I will jump off a cliff,
Into the lake.

BRIDGER DITTMER
GRADE 1

The Cliffs. **GARY ERTTER**

Air lies still,
Smelling of fresh pine.

KATIE McDANIEL
GRADE 9

Ponderosa Park. **TRIXI HUISH**

The Old Mill Site, McCall. **SANDRA COTTRELL**

Charlie's Garden. **GARY ERTTER**

The path for the gardener's work
Weaves among branch and bush
Creating a woven quilt of Spring.

ALINA EVERETT
GRADE 10

Ponderosa Park huckleberries. **MOLLY ELDREDGE**

Picking huckleberries is slow like a snail.
Picking huckleberries is messy like mud.
Huckleberry picking is like swimming
Through a bunch of bushes.

ALEXANDRA AMORT
GRADE 5

Kirby barn, Clear Creek. **HOWARD HAMILTON**

I love to hike in the mountains and
see all of the colorful wildflowers.

HANNA VEAL
GRADE 3

Upper Hazard Lake hike. **JOY HAMILTON**

Finnish sauna in Valley County. **NICKI HUMPHRIES**

Two geese looking. **HOWARD HAMILTON**

As the sun fades through the sky
between the staggered mountains,
the joy of Spring has begun.

CHRISTINE ROBERTS
GRADE 8

Old truck in flowers, Clear Creek.   **HOWARD HAMILTON**

Bright colors fill the world now
Making it all new.

ALYSSA AMORT
GRADE 9

Mule deer fawn. BARBARA EVANS

Lupine meadow, Elo Road, McCall. **MAGGIE ROSENTHAL**

Broad-tailed hummingbird with delphinium flowers. **TED DEMETRIADES**

Dense forests burst green
Flowers filled with soft humming
So it begins again.

SAM RAINEY
GRADE 9

Glorious waters,
Sunset in the sky,
Red, orange,
Fish jumping up high.

JESSICA WEISKIRCHER
GRADE 4

Sunset on Payette Lake, McCall. **HOWARD HAMILTON**

Epic air at Tamarack Resort. **SHERRI HARKIN**

Zooming through the day, zooming through the night,
I zoom on my bike day and night.

LEAH ANDERSON
GRADE 2

Like soldiers rushing to battle,
Mosquitoes surround me,
Thousands of little feet tickle my skin.

ERIN COYLE
GRADE 11

High mountain camping. **GARY ERTTER**

Aspen trees absorb water,
Bringing life to thirsty branches
Spring has at last arrived.

KATIE MCDANIEL
GRADE 9

Ponderosa State Park. **TED DEMETRIADES**

Payette Lake,
Majestic and still,
Coaxing, relaxing, welcoming.

ABIGAIL ACKERSON
GRADE 8

Payette Lake, McCall. **TED DEMETRIADES**

Whitetail Lodge, McCall. **TRIXI HUISH**

Whitetail Lodge, McCall.

Golf course at Whitetail.

Whitetail golf course clubhouse.

Water skiing on Payette Lake, McCall. © STEVE BLY \ IDAHO STOCK IMAGES

It feels like a fresh morning bath
in icy cold water to wake me up.

CELESTIAL PORTER
GRADE 5

Summer.
It is a busy rush
A mad dash to the beach
Running, splashing, fun.

SKYLER GULLICKSON
GRADE 9

Beach fun, Payette Lake. **COURTESY OF WHITETAIL CLUB & RESORT**

Tubing on Payette Lake. **MARIANNE EVENHUIS**

I feel the rush of wind against my face.
Water sprays into my eyes.
I feel the joy of speed.

DINA WILLIAMS
GRADE 6

Effortlessly, like a dragon, I carve monstrous turns,
leaving fascinating designs, swirling in the snow behind me.

IAN FAUROT
GRADE 12

Above: Classic Nordic race, Tamarack Resort. **SHERRI HARKIN**

Facing page: Powder skiing at Tamarack Resort. **SHERRI HARKIN**

Telemark roll, Brundage Mountain. **GARY ERTTER**

I love to ski.
My skis rip through the snow,
Zoom past trees,
My skis skip off jumps.

TANNER BORGESON
GRADE 2

I was doing ninety-five miles per hour
On a 700 Ski-doo
With no goggles
Powder flying in my face.

NORMAN ZIMMERMAN
GRADE 8

Valley County. ROBERT MONROE

Nordic race, Ponderosa Park. NICKI HUMPHRIES

Cougar Island, Payette Lake. **GARY ERTTER**

Quiet.
I close my eyes to isolate the soft sounds of the lake.
"Paradise," I whisper,
Without disturbing the beauty in my mind.

MICHAEL LIMBERT
GRADE 8

Look, Mom, that barn is falling down.

JOHN SABALA JR.
KINDERGARTEN

Fall rain, McCall. **JOY HAMILTON**

The fallen leaf is a rainbow on the ground.
The raindrop is a diamond fallen down.

SHANE VEAL
GRADE 1

Tired farm house off Highway 55. **JOY HAMILTON**

Mr. and Mrs. Huckleberry topiary sculptures. **TED DEMETRIADES**

Flight of Fancy, Donnelly. **SALLY DEMASI**

Main Street, Cascade. **MIKE HUSTON**

Historical Main Street, Cascade. **COURTESY OF TIM GARBER**

A scene flashes through my mind,
Frightful fumes fill the air,
No sweet sounds of birds
Or the whisper of a plant.

ERIN COYLE
GRADE 11

Blackwell fire, August 1994. TED DEMETRIADES

116

Smokejumpers "air attack," McCall. **GARY ERTTER**